The Circulatory System

by Rebecca Pettiford

BELLWETHER MEDIA • MINNEAPOLIS, MN

Note to Librarians, Teachers, and Parents:

Blastoff! Readers are carefully developed by literacy experts and combine standards-based content with developmentally appropriate text.

Level 1 provides the most support through repetition of high-frequency words, light text, predictable sentence patterns, and strong visual support.

Level 2 offers early readers a bit more challenge through varied simple sentences, increased text load, and less repetition of high-frequency words.

Level 3 advances early-fluent readers toward fluency through increased text and concept load, less reliance on visuals, longer sentences, and more literary language.

Level 4 builds reading stamina by providing more text per page, increased use of punctuation, greater variation in sentence patterns, and increasingly challenging vocabulary.

Level 5 encourages children to move from "learning to read" to "reading to learn" by providing even more text, varied writing styles, and less familiar topics.

Whichever book is right for your reader, Blastoff! Readers are the perfect books to build confidence and encourage a love of reading that will last a lifetime!

This edition first published in 2020 by Bellwether Media, Inc.

No part of this publication may be reproduced in whole or in part without written permission of the publisher. For information regarding permission, write to Bellwether Media, Inc., Attention: Permissions Department, 6012 Blue Circle Drive, Minnetonka, MN 55343.

Library of Congress Cataloging-in-Publication Data

Names: Pettiford, Rebecca, author.
Title: The Circulatory System / by Rebecca Pettiford.
Description: Minneapolis, MN : Bellwether Media, Inc., 2020. | Series:
   Blastoff! Readers. Your Body Systems | Audience: Age 5-8. | Audience: K to
   grade 3. | Includes bibliographical references and index.
Identifiers: LCCN 2018056089 (print) | LCCN 2018057531 (ebook) | ISBN
   9781618915597 (ebook) | ISBN 9781644870181 (hardcover : alk. paper) | ISBN
   9781618917515 (pbk. : alk. paper)
Subjects: LCSH: Cardiovascular system–Juvenile literature. | Heart–Juvenile
   literature.
Classification: LCC QP103 (ebook) | LCC QP103 .P377 2020 (print) | DDC
   612.1–dc23
LC record available at https://lccn.loc.gov/2018056089

Editor: Rebecca Sabelko   Designer: Brittany McIntosh

Printed in the United States of America, North Mankato, MN.

Table of Contents

What Is the Circulatory System?

blowing out carbon dioxide

The circulatory system carries **oxygen** and **nutrients** through the body. It also removes waste like **carbon dioxide**.

The system includes the heart, blood, and **blood vessels**.

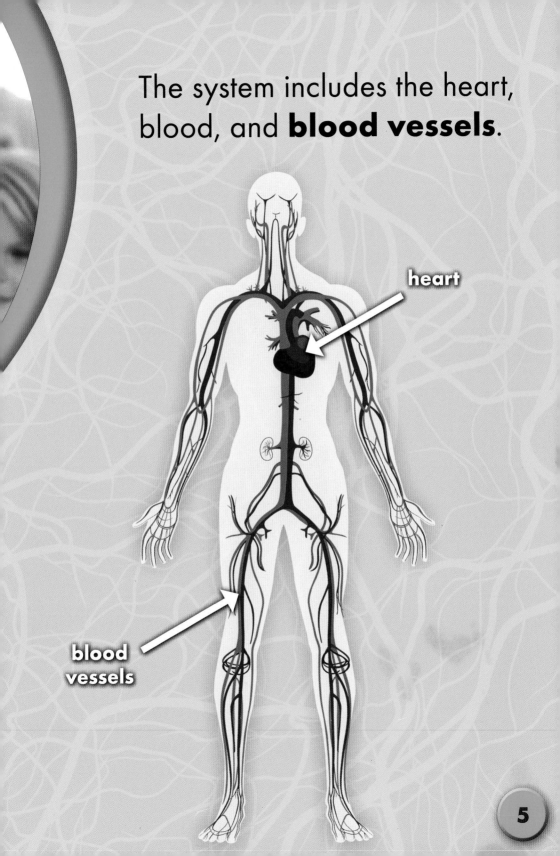

heart

blood vessels

The system begins and ends in the heart. The heart is a **muscle**. It pumps blood through the body.

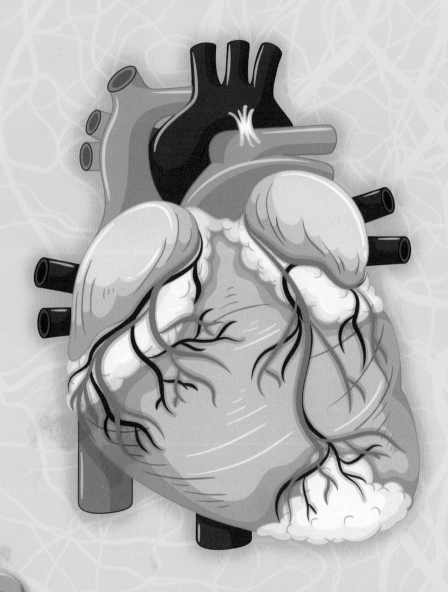

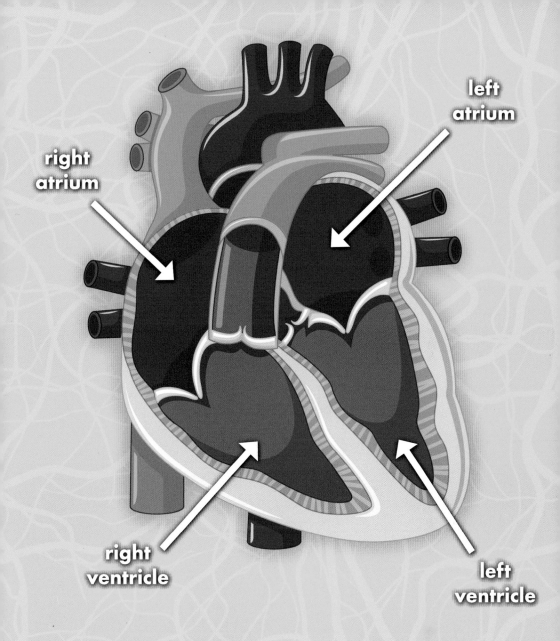

right atrium

left atrium

right ventricle

left ventricle

The heart has four **chambers**. The two upper chambers are the **atriums**. The two lower chambers are the **ventricles**.

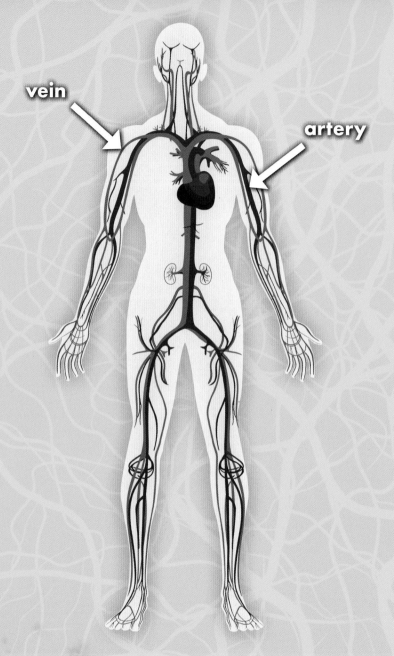

vein

artery

Two types of blood vessels carry blood. **Arteries** carry oxygen-rich blood away from the heart.

Veins carry waste-filled blood to the heart.

artery carrying oxygen-rich blood

How Does the Circulatory System Work?

Oxygen enters the lungs with a breath. Then the oxygen moves into the blood.

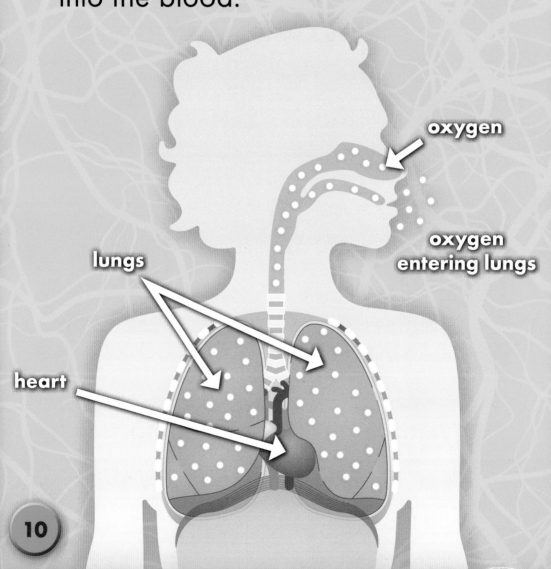

oxygen

oxygen entering lungs

lungs

heart

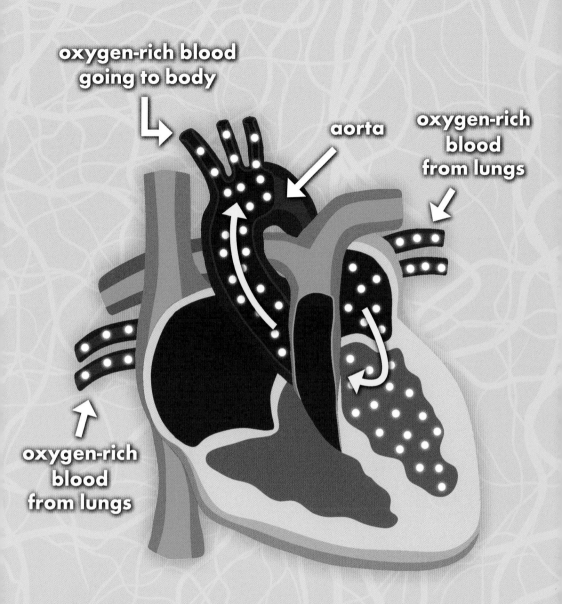

oxygen-rich blood
going to body

aorta

oxygen-rich
blood
from lungs

oxygen-rich
blood
from lungs

Arteries move this blood into the
left side of the heart. The heart
pumps the blood into the **aorta**.

The aorta branches into smaller arteries and **capillaries**. They carry the blood to the body's cells.

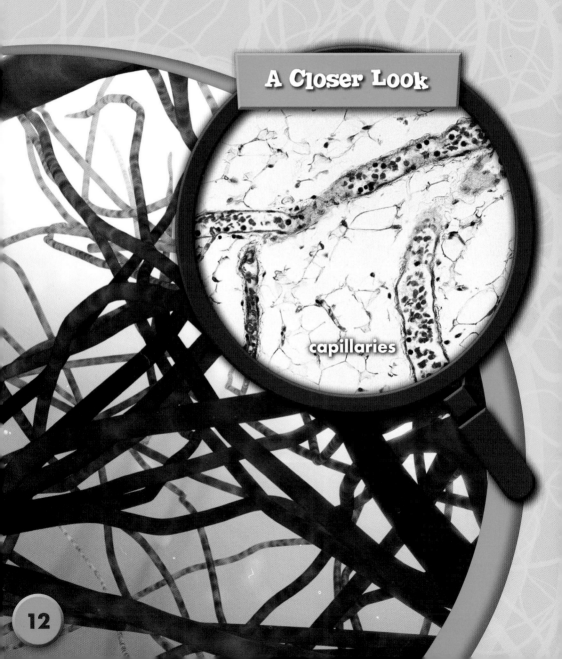

A Closer Look

capillaries

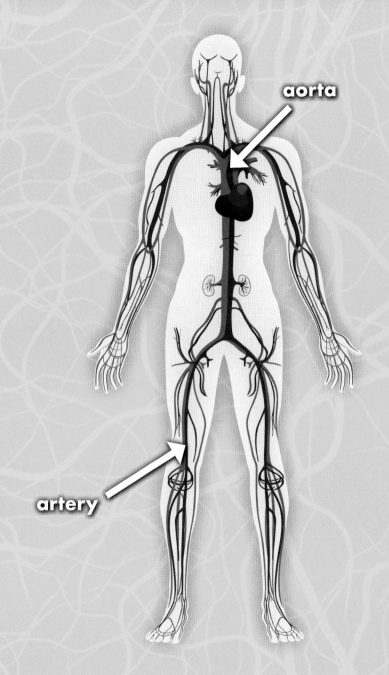

aorta

artery

The body's cells use the oxygen
and make waste. The waste begins
its journey to leave the body.

Blood in the capillaries picks up the waste. The blood moves into veins.

waste-filled blood in vein moving to heart

oxygen

waste

capillaries

oxygen-rich blood in artery moving through body

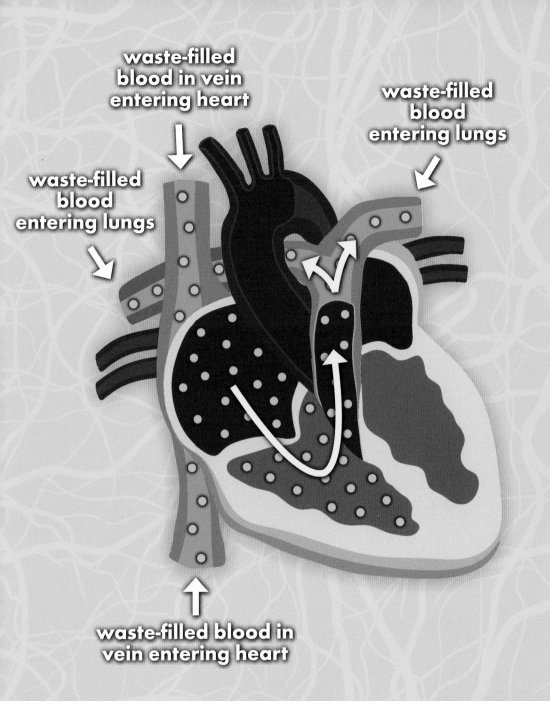

waste-filled blood in vein entering heart

waste-filled blood entering lungs

waste-filled blood entering lungs

waste-filled blood in vein entering heart

The veins take the blood to the right side of the heart.

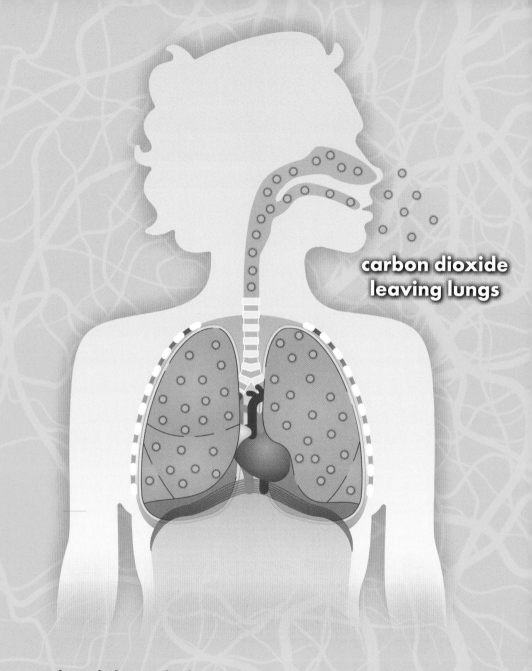

carbon dioxide leaving lungs

The blood then moves into the lungs. Carbon dioxide is breathed out.

The next breath brings in more oxygen. The cycle continues with each breath!

Why Is the Circulatory System Important?

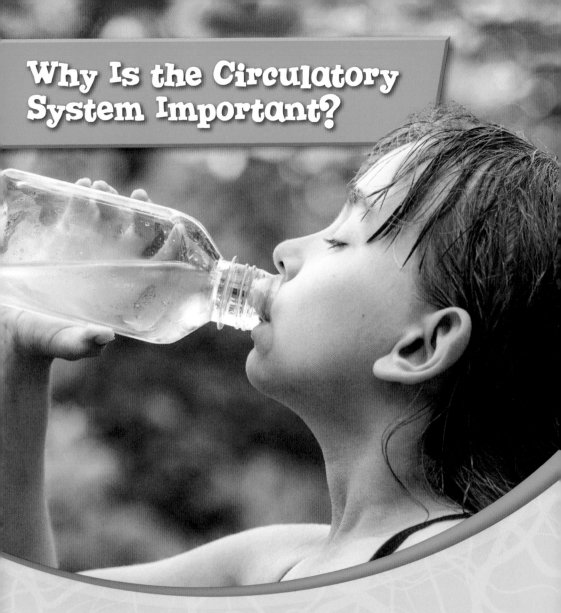

A healthy circulatory system keeps the body at the right temperature. This helps keep all body systems running.

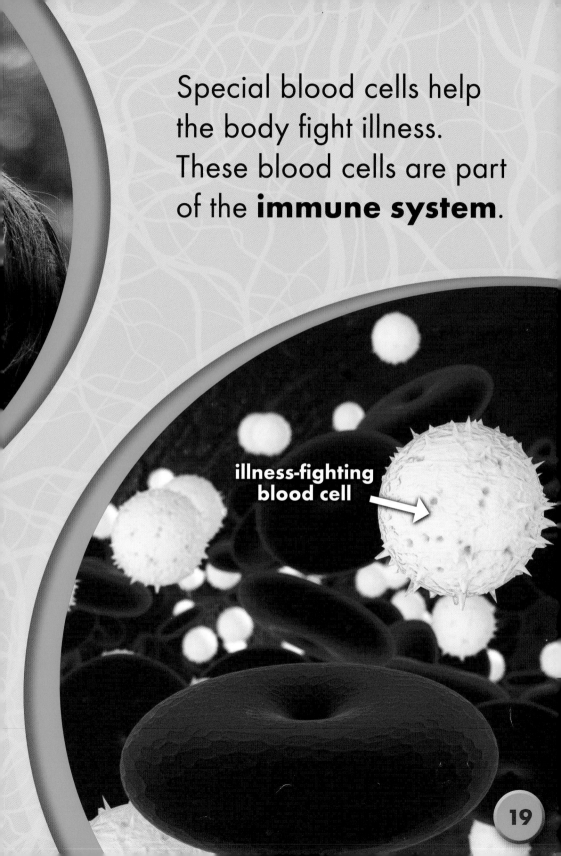

Special blood cells help
the body fight illness.
These blood cells are part
of the **immune system**.

illness-fighting
blood cell

Having a healthy heart keeps oxygen moving through the body. This is why it is important to exercise and eat right. The circulatory system keeps the body's cells alive!

Your Circulatory System at Work!

You can feel your heart beat as a pulse in your wrist.

You will need:
- a stopwatch
- a pen or pencil
- a notepad

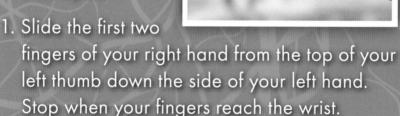

1. Slide the first two fingers of your right hand from the top of your left thumb down the side of your left hand. Stop when your fingers reach the wrist.

2. Slide your fingers down until you feel a tendon. It feels like a thin rope.

3. When you find a steady beat, count the number of beats in one minute. Record your resting pulse rate.

4. Now run or do jumping jacks for one minute. Record your pulse rate for one minute.

5. Rest for one minute. Record your pulse rate again.

How does your pulse change?

Glossary

aorta—the largest artery in the body

arteries—blood vessels that carry blood from the heart to all parts of the body

atriums—the two upper chambers of the heart

blood vessels—small tubes that carry blood to and from all parts of the body

capillaries—the smallest blood vessels that deliver oxygen to the body's cells; capillaries connect arteries and veins.

carbon dioxide—a gas that people breathe out; cells make carbon dioxide.

chambers—areas in the heart; the human heart has four chambers.

immune system—the system that protects the body from illness

muscle—a body tissue that helps move parts of the body

nutrients—the things humans need to live and grow

oxygen—a gas in the air that is necessary for life; people breathe in oxygen.

veins—blood vessels that carry blood back to the heart

ventricles—the two lower chambers of the heart

To Learn More

AT THE LIBRARY

Bassington, Cyril. *Your Heart*. New York, N.Y.: Gareth Stevens Publishing, 2017.

Cole, Taylor. *The Circulatory System*. New York, N.Y.: Gareth Stevens Publishing, 2019.

Kenney, Karen Latchana. *Circulatory System*. Minneapolis, Minn.: Jump!, 2017.

ON THE WEB

FACTSURFER

Factsurfer.com gives you a safe, fun way to find more information.

1. Go to www.factsurfer.com.

2. Enter "circulatory system" into the search box and click 🔍.

3. Select your book cover to see a list of related web sites.

Index

The images in this book are reproduced through the courtesy of: mdgrphcs, front cover; Monkey Business Images, p. 4; Vecton, pp. 5, 8, 13; GraphicsRF, pp. 6, 7, 11, 15; nobeastsofierce, p. 9; VectorMine, pp. 10, 16; Image Source/ Alamy, p. 12 (top); Design_Cells, p. 12 (bottom); BlueRingMedia, p. 14; islandboy, p. 17; bigandt.com, p. 18; Immersion Imagery, p. 19; Jacek Chabraszewski, p. 20; caimacanul, p. 21.